FUTURE SCIENCE NOW!

WHAT'S NEXT FOR THE ENVIRONMENT?

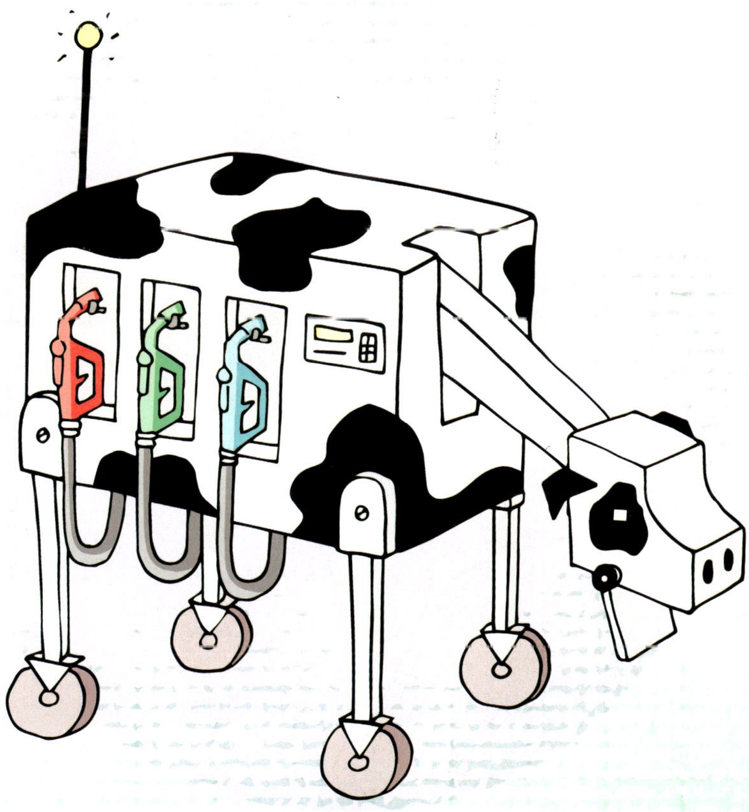

Tom Jackson

WAYLAND

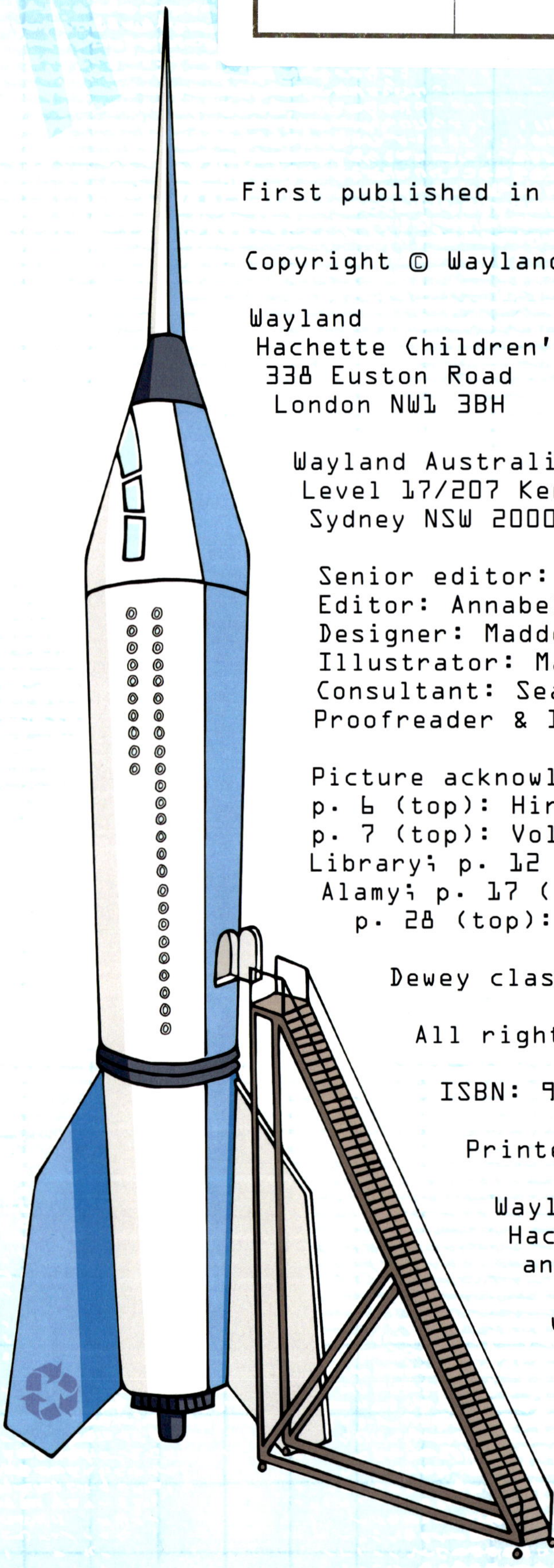

First published in 2013 by Wayland

Wayland
Hachette Children's Books
338 Euston Road
London NW1 3BH

Wayland Australia
Level 17/207 Kent Street
Sydney NSW 2000

Senior editor: Julia Adams
Editor: Annabel Stones
Designer: Maddox Philpot
Illustrator: Maddox Philpot
Consultant: Sean Connolly
Proofreader & Indexer: Kay Barnham

Picture acknowledgements:
p. 6 (top): Hiroshi Watanabe/Getty Images; p. 7 (top): Volker Steger/Science Photo Library; p. 12 (bottom): AlamyCelebrity/Alamy; p. 17 (bottom): Kevpix/Alamy; p. 28 (top): Visuals Unlimited/Corbis

Dewey classification: 333.7

ISBN: 978 0 7502 7798 3

Printed in China

Wayland is a division of Hachette Children's Books, an Hachette UK Company.

www.hachette.co.uk

Environment science now 04
The home 06
Power supplies 08
New fuels 10
Getting around 12
Making long journeys 14
In the future city 16
Waste time 18
Growing food 20
Conservation 22
Climate challenges 24
Health and safety 26
Copying nature 28
Glossary and useful websites 30
Index 32

EVIRONMENT SCIENCE NOW

What do we mean by the word 'environment'? It can refer to everything around you, from the conditions inside a house to natural landscapes across an entire continent. Whichever environment we are talking about, we need to look after it – after all, it is where we live.

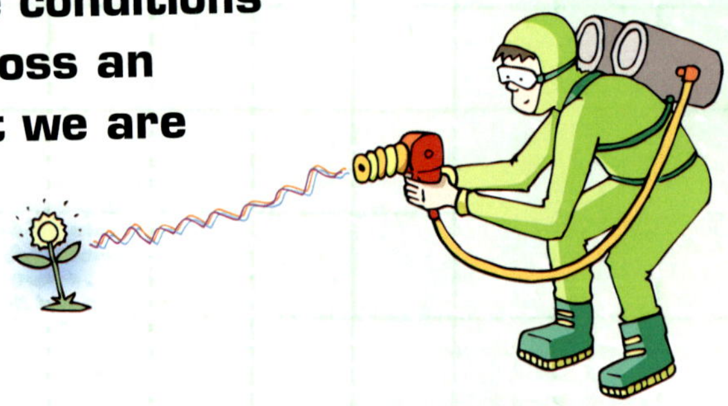

Natural Habitats

A natural habitat is a type of environment that grows all by itself. Everyone agrees that natural landscapes are pleasant places and people like to visit the countryside. However, farmers' fields are not actually that natural. Over the years, natural woodlands, wetlands and meadows have been cleared to make land for growing our food. Maintaining the right balance between farmland and natural wilderness will be one of the big challenges for the future.

BUILT ENVIRONMENT

Houses, towns and the transport networks (such as roads and railways) that connect them are also part of the environment. While other animals are restricted in where they live – camels like the desert, polar bears stay in the Arctic – human technology allows us to live just about anywhere. We are the only species to live on all seven of Earth's continents. The last one that we have inhabited is Antarctica – there has been a permanent settlement there since 1956. Where might we move next?

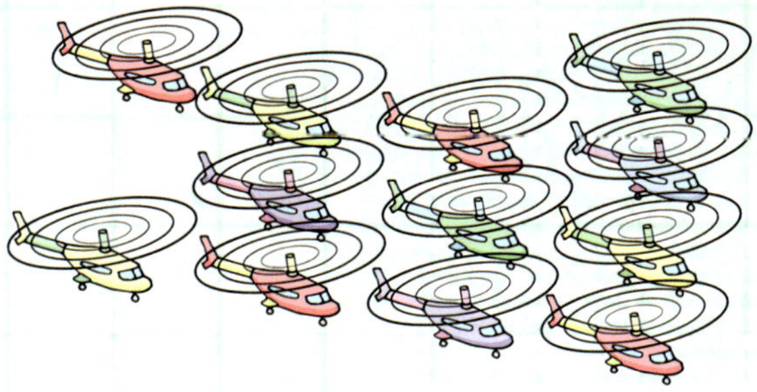

Power supply

Since the dawn of civilisation, humans have needed fuels and a power supply. At first this was to provide some heat and light and to cook food. Today we use it for many more things – the list is very long indeed. It has taken less than 150 years (the first power station was built in Germany in 1878) for 80% of the world to be supplied with electricity. However, one billion people still do not have any power supply at all – how will we get clean, safe energy to them?

Into the future

Half of everyone on Earth lives in a city, and more people are moving in from the countryside every day. The future of the environment has some big problems. In this book we'll look at the latest research and scientific developments and explore how they might change the way we live in the years to come. An icon next to each technology we introduce will give you an idea of when they may become a part of our daily lives.

THE HOME

Despite all the advances in technology over the years, the place where we sleep, eat and relax – our home – has not changed very much for many centuries and neither has the furniture in it. However, new technology is always trying to improve things.

House HQ

10 YEARS

It is quite normal now for our electronic gadgets - phones, music players and TVs - to connect to each other. Eventually everything in the house - from the lights and heating to the curtains, front door and shopping list - will be connected to a home network. Where would you put the main control panel? Under the stairs or in a high-tech control room? The most likely place will be a touchscreen in the kitchen.

The control centre of a future house.

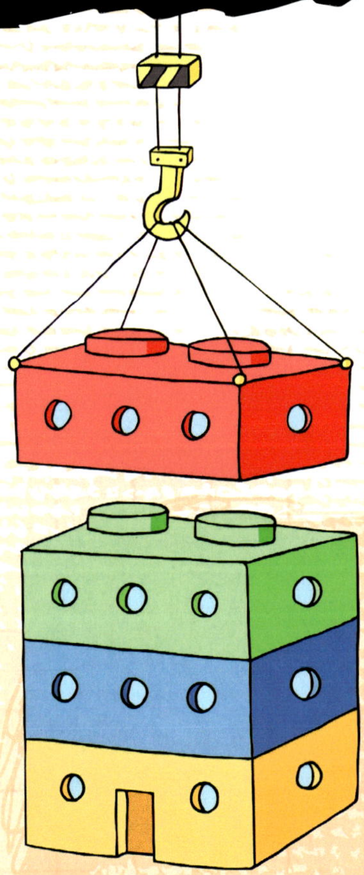

Cocoon bed

15 YEARS

Why have a bedroom and a living room, when you can merge them both into one super comfy cocoon? In future, people will retreat to cosy pods, where they can sit comfortably to read, watch videos, or chat with friends online. At bedtime, we will just lie down to sleep. The lighting and temperature are all controlled from inside the cocoon, and that saves energy, because we are heating just the cocoon, not the whole room.

Room stacks

20 YEARS

Building a new house or making an old one bigger and better is very expensive - and there is often no space to do it. In future, houses will be constructed like modelling blocks. You just choose your rooms and connect them together. If you need a new room it will arrive from a factory - already built to be environmentally friendly - and hoisted into place.

COMPUTER COMPANIONS

20 YEARS

In future, the house might be another member of the family, or at least an AI computer (AI stands for artificial intelligence) that understands voice commands from the human residents. It uses face recognition to tell where everyone is and could hold a conversation with them, playing and joking with the kids and discussing housekeeping with the adults.

Flat OLEDs will also be used in screens.

Plastic lights

5 YEARS

In the house of the future just about anything could be made of light bulbs. Organic light-emitting diodes (OLEDs) are layers of plastic and organic chemicals that light up when electrified. (Organic means 'based on life', and organic chemicals are made up mainly of carbon and hydrogen atoms, like the chemicals in a living body.) OLEDs produce a lot of light, but do not get hot. You could also tune them to show the perfect colour and brightness of light – to help you relax or wake your up in the morning.

IT'S ELEMENTARY

Spirals of light

Low-energy light bulbs are fluorescent tubes that contain gases which glow when they are electrified. They give out less heat than old-fashioned bulbs, which wasted energy by getting very hot. Fluorescent tubes are not a new invention, but the original tube lights were too long for homes. The compact fluorescent bulbs we use today are coiled into a helix, or 3D spiral. That shape takes up less room but still allows the light produced to escape into the room.

POWER SUPPLIES

Technology is great at making our lives easier, saving us time and creating a safe and comfortable place to live. However, the big drawback is that it all needs to be powered in some way – and that uses up valuable energy resources and can cause serious environmental problems. In future our gadgets will need more efficient power supplies.

GEOTHERMAL LASER DRILLING

10 YEARS

It is warm underground. The temperature goes up by 1°C every 40 m. This means that about 4 km into Earth's crust the rock is hot enough to boil water - and that is all we need to generate electricity. There are 'geothermal' (meaning 'Earth heat') plants working today near volcanoes, where the heat is close to the surface. Drilling deep enough into normal rock is almost impossible with today's equipment. However, a high-powered laser drill is being developed that cracks up rocks with a super-hot flash of heat, which could make deep drilling easier and mean that geothermal power is available all over the world.

Pulling power

5 YEARS

Gravity is everywhere. It is the force that keeps our feet on the ground – and stops us flying off into space. The same pull can be harnessed to power a light bulb and in future might be used on other things like phone chargers or computers. The gravity power source has to be hung above the ground with a bag of sand or rocks hooked to it. To start the device running, you raise the bag and let go – and gravity takes over. The weight of the bag pulls on gears inside, turning an electricity generator, and powers the light.

Growing oil

10 YEARS

Plants are nature's solar power stations. They trap the energy in sunlight and make it into sugar in a process called photosynthesis (see page 21). One day we could use pools of blue-green algae – microscopic photosynthesising bugs – to grow a fuel. On sunny days the algae grow rapidly into a oozy sludge, filled with an energy-rich oil. Unlike petrol and coal, this farmed fuel does not add extra carbon dioxide to the atmosphere when it is burned. In fact the process could take out more carbon than it puts back in.

Solar flannels

3 YEARS

We could charge our portable devices – phones and tablets – using a portable solar panel. These will be made of flexible material that can be rolled or folded away when not being used. We could even have sun hats made from the same material to keep us cool while charging our mobile phones!

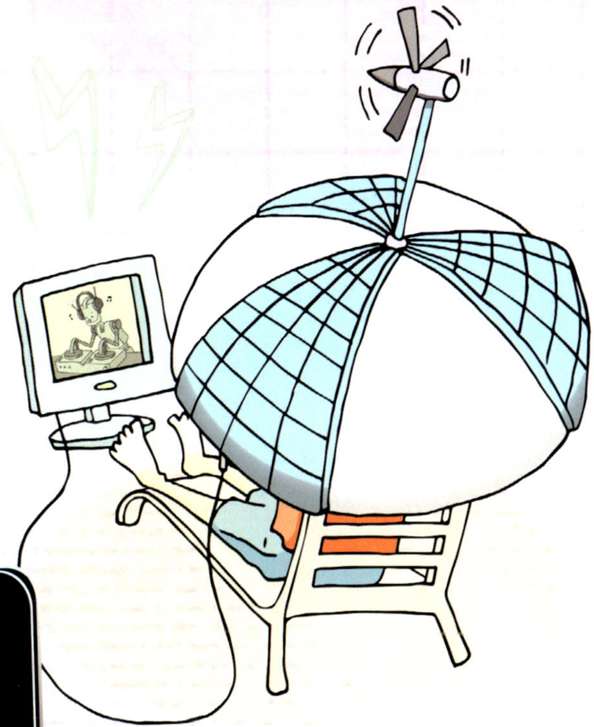

IT'S ELEMENTARY

From flow to spin

When a magnet and metal wire move past each other, their motion produces an electric current inside the wire. A power station generates electricity by spinning wires around inside strong magnets. That spinning motion is delivered by a fan-shaped machine called a turbine. The job of the turbine is to convert a forward motion into a spinning motion. The forward motion could come from the wind, the flow of a river or be a stream of super-hot steam produced by burning coal or gas. The moving gas or liquid hits the turbine blades, making them spin.

Tidal reef

20 YEARS

The tides roll in and out like clockwork and all that moving water could be harnessed to produce huge amounts of electricity. The problem is building power plants that are tough enough to withstand ocean storms and stay working in the cold salty water. One idea is to build an artificial reef at the mouth of a river. Instead of coral or rock, they would be made of concrete blocks that sit just below the surface at low tide. As the tide floods in, the water surges up and over the reef and through turbines sitting on top. Unlike a dam, a tidal reef won't block the river and lets wildlife swim through.

NEW FUELS

The fuels we use today – coal, natural gas and oil – were formed over millions of years from the remains of long-dead plants and other life forms. That is why we sometimes call them fossil fuels. Fossil fuels contain carbon, which burns with oxygen, giving out the heat and light that we need. But it also dumps carbon dioxide gas, taken out of the air all those years ago, back into the atmosphere. This extra gas is causing dangerous climate changes. We need new sources of fuel – and fast.

Burning ice

10 YEARS

There are thick layers of natural gas, called methane, in the frozen ground of the Arctic Circle. This frozen gas is called clathrate and, once at the surface, a chunk of this icy chemical can be set on fire! Although it is still a fossil fuel, experts suggest that burning clathrate ice (and turning it into carbon dioxide) might be better than letting it melt and give out methane gas. That is because methane gas in the atmosphere could upset the climate even more than carbon dioxide.

Hydrogen balls

30 YEARS

Pure hydrogen is a highly flammable gas and, unlike fossil fuels, when it burns it produces nothing but harmless steam. Why not use hydrogen as a fuel? The problem is that hydrogen explodes very easily. One tiny leak, and BANG, you get a very big problem. Trapping it inside hollow glass balls could make it safer. The balls are so small that one thousand lined up would measure less than 1 mm. That makes them small enough to be pumped through pipes like a liquid. The engine would suck the fuel gas out of the balls only when it was time to burn it.

Fuelling factory

15 YEARS

Ammonia is a chemical made of hydrogen and nitrogen. Although it is poisonous, it may one day replace petrol. Liquid ammonia burns to make nothing but steam and nitrogen, a harmless gas already in the atmosphere. Ammonia is currently made in huge chemical plants, which mix gases at high temperatures. As the starting materials are water and air, one day mini chemical plants at every filling station could be making their own ammonia and pumping it straight into cars.

PAUSE FOR THOUGHT

The system for making ammonia is called the Haber process. It reacts nitrogen (from the air) with hydrogen gas. The process was developed by German Fritz Haber in 1909. Plants need to take nitrogen-rich chemicals from the soil, and the Haber process makes it possible to manufacture chemical fertilizers, which boost our ability to grow food, in factories. However, the Haber process also makes it easier to make powerful explosives, too. Half of all the food we grow today is due to fertilizers made from ammonia. But without ammonia, the world wars of the 20th century would not have lasted more than a few months, saving millions of lives. Is the Haber process a good thing?

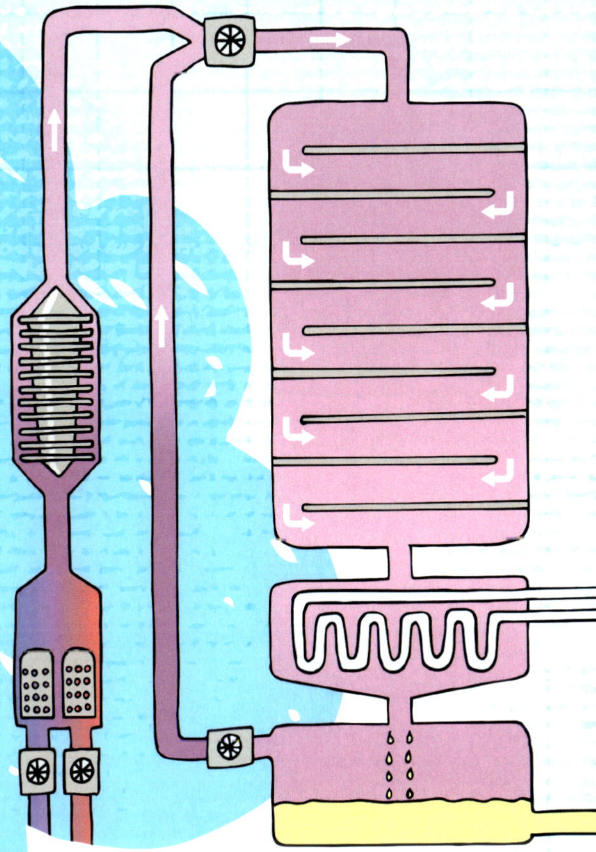

Self-feeding vehicles

30 YEARS

We may never have to refuel our cars if self-feeding engines become common. Robot vehicles that 'eat' grasses and plants are being developed. They will cut down plants and load them into a 'stomach' that ferments them into fuels like alcohol and methane. Of course, if everyone had one of these robots, the planet might soon run out of plants.

GETTING AROUND

Today we might nip out in the car to the shops, catch a bus to school, or cycle to work – or even walk. Most of us make short journeys every day so what can science do to help us get around in future?

'Copter swarms

Even today, in the world's biggest cities, some people never travel on the ground. They fly instead, making short trips between the helipads on the rooftops of super-tall skyscrapers. As the number of helicopters increases, city skies will get as crowded as the roads below. An air-traffic system is being developed that organises helicopters into 'swarms' or formations that fly safely across the city – always staying out of each other's way.

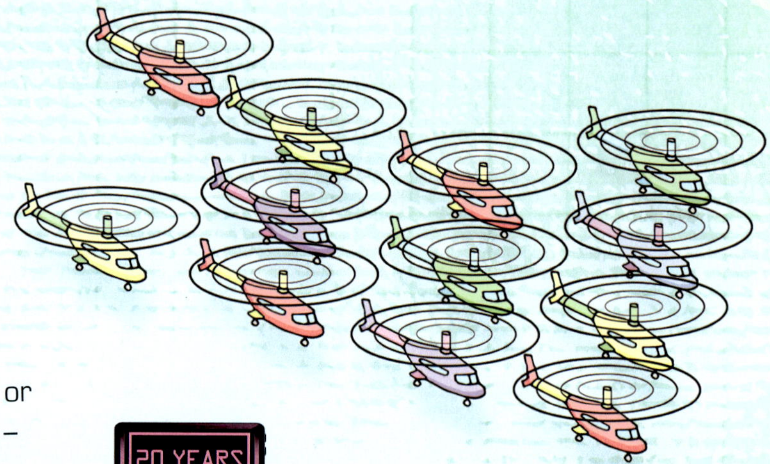

20 YEARS

Prototype Shweebs are tested out.

Driverless cars

10 YEARS

It might sound odd but if people let their cars drive themselves it will be safer. The cars will sense their surroundings using laser-powered distance finders, mini radars and cameras. Every computer driver will calculate the positions of all road users and know when to stop and start safely - and it can always find the best route through heavy traffic. (There have been driverless car races in the Nevada Desert; the only people are the spectators.)

Pedal pod

5 YEARS

Cycling around is a good way to keep fit and does not produce pollution. Railways are a great way of moving large numbers of people around a city. The Shweeb combines both - recumbent bikes (you lie back on them) hang from a monorail that weaves through the city, high above the roads and rivers that get in the way at street level. Just hop on at your local Shweeb stop and pedal to your destination.

Self-balancing car-bike

5 YEARS

Two-wheeled bikes take up less room than four-wheeled cars. If we all rode bikes then there would be more room on the roads and fewer traffic jams. However, it is much easier to fall off a motorbike so most people prefer cars. In future we could use car-bikes instead. They will be enclosed, have two wheels, one or two seats and a self-balancing system that makes riding safer. Gyroscopes inside detect every movement and keep the car-bike safely balanced, even tilting it as it whizzes around corners.

IT'S ELEMENTARY

In a spin

A gyroscope is a relatively simple device, a bit like a spinning top. Once it is spinning it always maintains its angular momentum – that means it keeps the same position, even when everything else around it has moved. For example, gyroscopes are used inside an aircraft to show if it is flying upwards, downwards, or straight and level.

Ride the roller coaster

15 YEARS

City rail networks have something to learn from roller-coaster rides. Roller coasters are all about the ups and downs. All the work is done pushing the cars to the very top and when they slide down the other side, their spinning wheels are used to recharge the motor, ready for the next circuit. Small elevated railways that might run between the tall buildings in a city of the future could take advantage of the same system. The track will have gentle rises and falls that make each journey as efficient as possible.

MAKING LONG JOURNEYS

Travelling around the world has never been easier. Within hours a family from Japan can arrive in Brazil, or fresh vegetables from Africa can be in shops in Scotland. In future long-distance travel will be even faster, but also produce less pollution and be more efficient.

SWIMMING FREIGHTERS

40 YEARS

Look around your house. Most of the objects you see will have been on a ship at some point on their way from the factory to the shop. In future, cargoships could be the largest robots in the world that find their way without a human captain. In 2012, the first robot ship sailed across the Pacific Ocean, from San Francisco, USA, to Queensland, Australia. It has no engine, but is powered by the action of the waves. It only moves slowly – the journey took all year – but in future non-urgent materials, like grain or sand, might be transported in huge versions of this clever ocean-goer.

Sailing super solar ships

10 YEARS

The largest container ships can carry as much cargo as 15,000 lorries – and they use 250 tonnes of fuel every day. Cargo ships might one day use an old trick to save on fuel – hoist some sails to catch the ocean winds. And by covering the sails with solar panels they could charge the engine batteries for when the wind drops – or the energy could be used to pump bubbles of air under the ship which would help the vessel glide though the water better.

Air highways

5 YEARS

Most of an aircraft's fuel is used to take off and land, especially at the busiest airports, where the skies are full of planes just flying around in circles, waiting to touch down. New air-traffic tracking systems that use satellites – not radar systems on the ground like we have now – will let air-traffic controllers know exactly where every plane is. That means aircraft will be allowed to fly on more direct routes, not along the 'flightpaths' watched by radar, which wastes fuel.

TELEPORTATION

100 YEARS

In future, scientists might be able to build teleporters that can zap an object from one place to another in the blink of an eye. The teleporter uses a super-cooled substance, which is so cold that its atoms have dissolved into a pool of simpler particles. The object being sent is plunged into this substance, and as its atoms collapse they give away all the energy that is holding them together. The idea is to send that energy signal along a cable to another teleporter (which could be anywhere). The receiving machine uses the energy to rebuild atoms by warming the super-cooled pool - and the object reappears! But even if this works, would anyone want to travel this way?

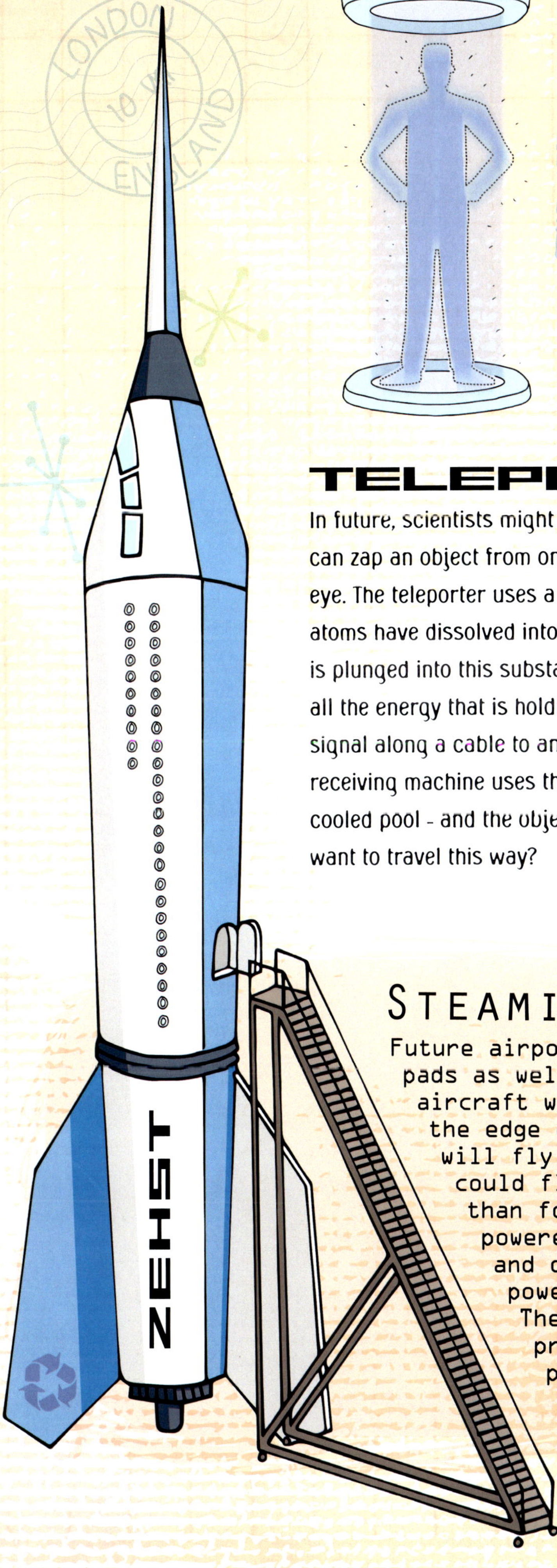

STEAMING AHEAD

20 YEARS

Future airports may have launch pads as well as runways. Passenger aircraft will take off like rockets and fly at the edge of space. The super-fast airliners will fly more than 1 km in a second and could fly halfway around the world in less than four hours. The aircraft will be powered by burning a mixture of hydrogen and oxygen gas just like the most powerful modern spacecraft do today. The best thing is that the exhaust gas produced by these supersonic rocket planes will be steam — they will not produce pollution.

IN THE FUTURE CITY

More than half of everyone on Earth lives in a city – and the number of city folk is going to keep going up for many more years. The advantage of a city is that everything is close by and convenient to get to. However, that also has its disadvantages, resulting in crowds, delays and a lot of mess. How will science make city living better in future?

Tsunami-proof towns

15 YEARS

We do like to be beside the seaside: the number of people living close to the ocean is higher than ever. This means that more and more people are in danger of being hit by super-storms or tsunamis in the future. In Japan, a place that has more tsunamis than most (the word itself is Japanese), it has been suggested that coastal towns should be built on walled islands raised above the rest of the landscape. Then, if a wave rushes in from the sea it will just flow around the town.

THE ROAD SOUTH

2 YEARS

An ice road is being built to the South Pole. It will connect ships that arrive on the edge of the ice sheet in spring with the research base at the very bottom of the globe. It will take 20 days to travel to the Pole – it is uphill for most of the journey – and 10 days to get back again. The road will only be open 100 days a year – but the sun never sets in that time, so traffic will run 24 hours a day. The road and a fat communication cable running alongside it will make the South Pole more like any other city with fast Internet connections and regular deliveries – although only frozen food is available.

PAUSE FOR THOUGHT

Antarctica is one of the last wildernesses on Earth. Until 1956, humans only visited for a few months at a time, and since then very few people live on the continent all year round. Is it a good thing to build roads and bigger settlements in Antarctica, or should we leave it empty?

Sky High

50 YEARS

In future entire cities could be contained in one huge building, hundreds of times bigger than the Great Pyramid, with room for hundreds of thousands of people. They could reach several kilometres into the sky – but at that height the air at the top is too thin to breathe (and it's very cold too). The building will be pressurised like an aircraft, so the air is the same wherever you are inside. Such a building is too heavy to build with today's construction materials, but one day super-strong components, made from tiny tubes of pure carbon (known as nanotubes) might make them possible.

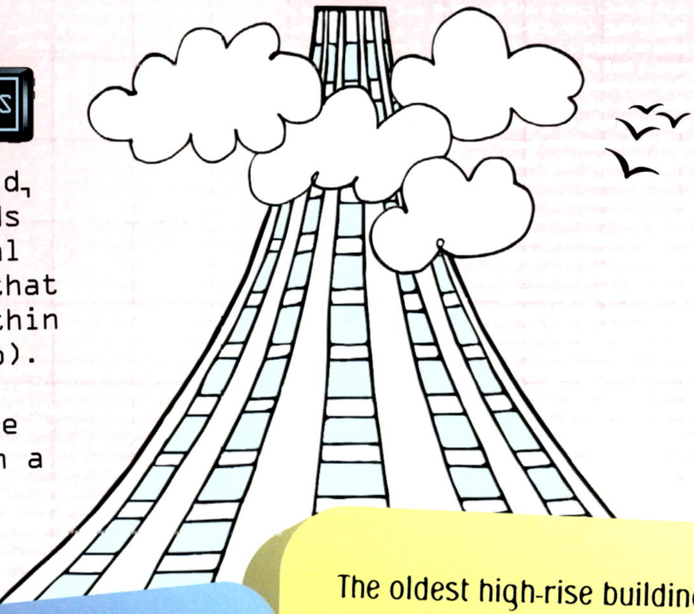

Stacks of Facts

The oldest high-rise buildings are in Sana'a in the Yemen; they have several storeys made of mud bricks. They date back 1,400 years to when the city centre got too crowded for new houses - so the old buildings just got taller.

A building made from bricks cannot go higher than 16 storeys. If it is any higher, the bricks begin to crack under the great weight.

The largest city on Earth is Tokyo-Yokohama in Japan. It used to be two cities but they got so big that they joined together; 39 million people live there.

Desert oasis

10 YEARS

A brand-new city is being built in Abu Dhabi. Masdar City is being designed to rely entirely on renewable energy. Solar panels will provide power during the day. All the rubbish will be burned and the heat it gives out used as an energy source. In the heat of the desert, buildings will be kept cool with air chilled inside towers by the wind. The streets and parks will be covered with wide parasols by day. At night these will fold down to let the city release its heat into the sky and cool down.

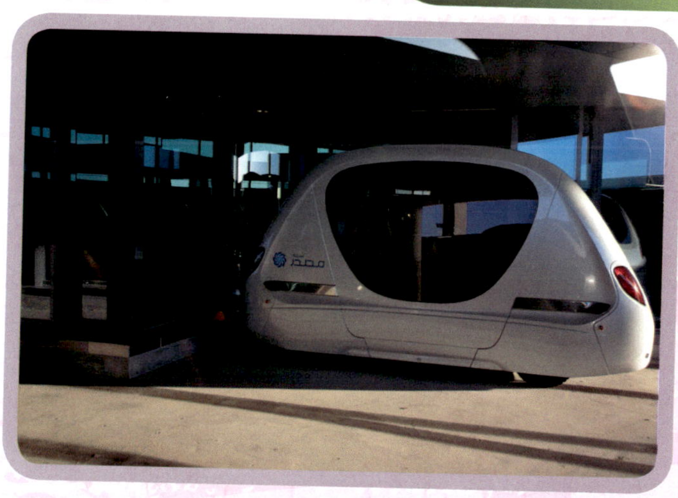

Masdar residents will travel around in electric driverless pods.

WASTE TIME

The average person in the UK produces seven times their own bodyweight in rubbish every year. Most of that gets buried in huge rubbish dumps called landfill sites. We'd better find a new way to reduce our rubbish or we'll run out of room very soon.

Recycling scanner

5 YEARS

The best way to cut down on landfill is to recycle our rubbish. If we sorted our waste into different materials - glass, plastic, cardboard etc - we could easily reuse three-quarters of it, maybe more! But often we can't be bothered and just chuck it away all mixed together. In future, scanners at waste-management sites will shine a beam of light - including colours we can't see like infrared and ultraviolet - on to the piles of rubbish. Different materials reflect certain colours, and so robot grabbers can be directed to sort the rubbish for us and recycle as much as possible.

VAPORISING WASTE

10 YEARS

Whatever we can't recycle does not have to be buried. It is quite common for rubbish to be burned, or incinerated, and it can even be used as a fuel for generating power. Older incinerators can produce nasty pollution, but in future we will burn rubbish using plasma – a blast of electrified gas hotter than the surface of the sun. All the waste (even sewage) would be turned to pretty harmless gases like steam and nitrogen.

Parking space

40 YEARS

Junk in space is a growing problem and it will only get worse as we launch more satellites into orbit. There are hundreds of thousands of bits of debris in orbit around our planet ranging from nuts and bolts to dead satellites. Rather than leaving these unused satellites to fall to Earth – and perhaps crash into active spacecraft – in future we might park them at a place in space called L1. This is a spot between Earth and the Moon where the gravitational pull from both cancels each other out. The space junk would stay safely at L1 for ever – or until it was collected by a recycling spacecraft.

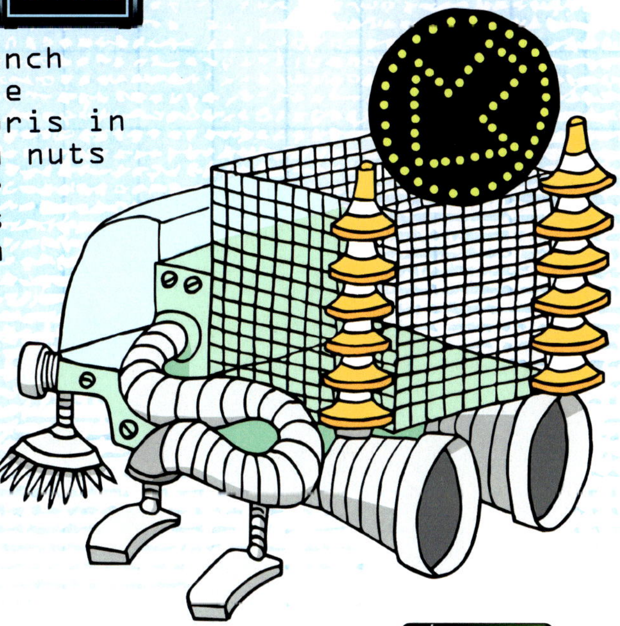

Drawing water

5 YEARS

Osmosis is a process that occurs when watery mixtures are separated by a membrane barrier. The membrane lets the water through but blocks large items, like mud or bacteria. The water moves across to even out the concentrations of the mixtures on both sides. Osmosis can be used to clean any water – even sewage – and might one day be a common system in places without a proper water supply. A bag (made of membrane) of very salty water is dunked into the dirty water. Pure water moves out of the dirty water, through a membrane and into the bag, leaving all the gunk behind. This means you have enough clean water to drink, but it will taste salty. The trick is to use ammonium bicarbonate salt. Heating up the water to just above body temperature makes the salt turn to gas and fizz out of the water, leaving a pure drink behind.

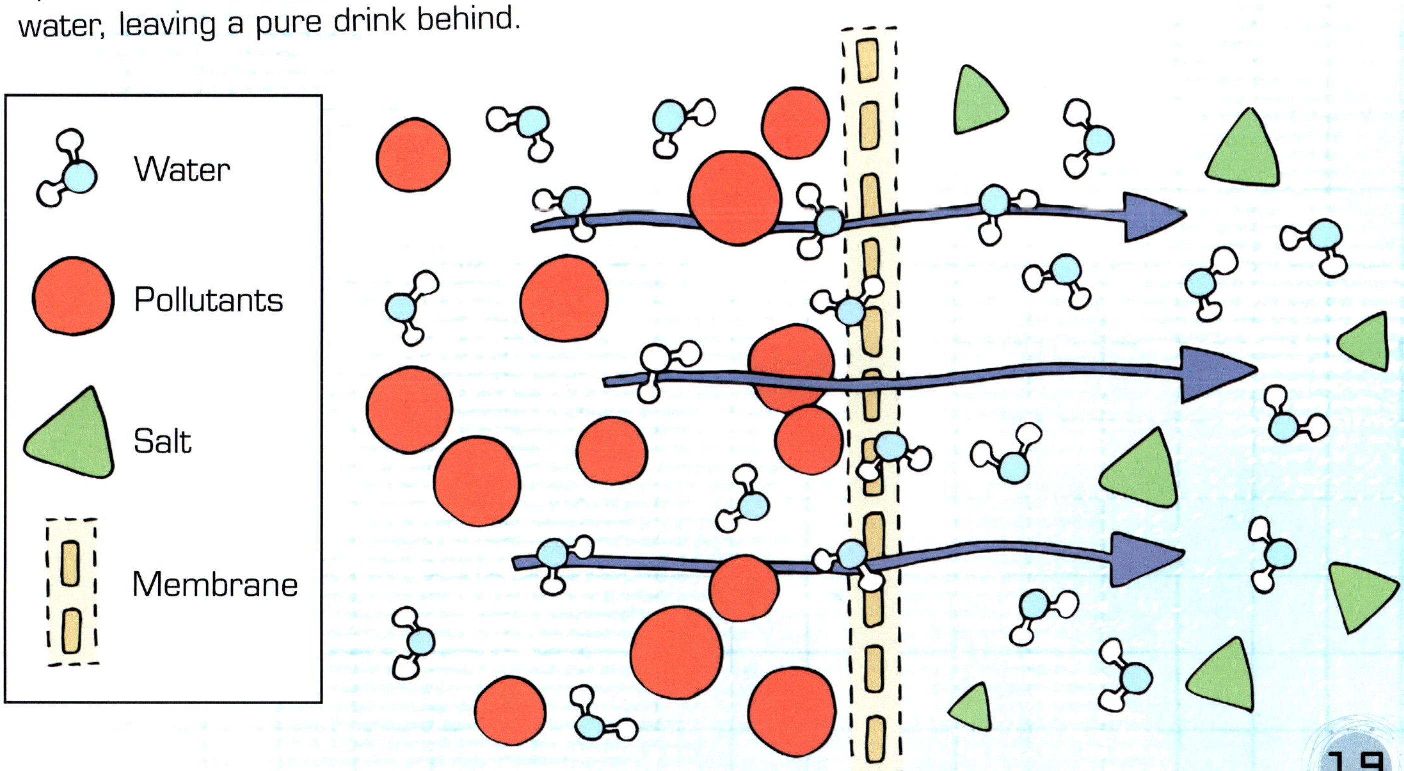

GROWING FOOD

The world's human population is gradually becoming healthier, wealthier, and living longer. This is good news, but at the same time the population is also growing, which creates another problem. By 2050 we will need to grow twice as much food as we do now. That's going to need some new farming technology.

Laser-guided weed killer

15 YEARS

Weeds are just plants that farmers don't like. The key to weeding is to kill the unwanted plants while leaving the crops untouched. A laser-guided weed gun fitted to tractors could do this automatically, using a scanner to recognise good and bad plants by the shapes of their leaves. When a weed comes into its sights, the gun targets a tiny squirt of weedkiller so precisely that no other plant is touched.

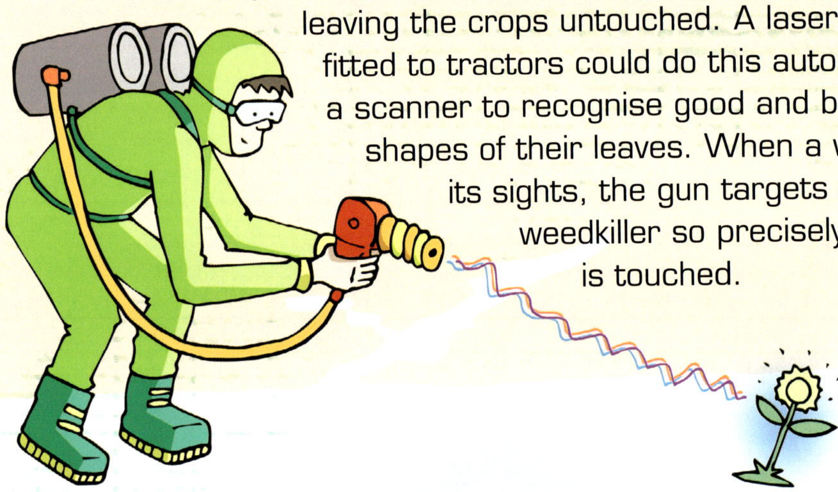

FARMBOTS

30 YEARS

Modern farms are already pretty high-tech. Tractors can steer themselves using satellite navigation and dairy cows are milked by robotic machines. However, today's big tractors might one day be replaced with fleets of smaller robot farmers, which sow seeds in tight geometric grids instead of wide furrows, scanning the colour of grains and fruits for the perfect ripeness. The farmbot will be much lighter than tractors, and so won't crush the soil. That saves energy while ploughing, leaves more room for crops and – unlike human farmers – they can work day or night.

BLACK PLANTS

20 YEARS

Plants do not eat to survive; instead they capture the energy in sunlight to make sugars. This process is called photosynthesis. The thing is, photosynthesis is not very efficient and in future we could engineer a better system so crops grow bigger, faster. Sunlight is trapped by chlorophyll in the leaves, which takes the red and blue light and reflects black the green – that is why leaves are green. A modified chlorophyll could absorb all the light, making use of every bit of its energy. But that would mean the leaves would appear black.

IT'S ELEMENTARY

Photosynthesis

The term photosynthesis means 'making with light'. Everything humans and all of the world's other animals eat has been produced directly or indirectly from photosynthesis – either we eat plants, or we eat an animal that has been eating them. Photosynthesis is a reaction between carbon dioxide gas (taken from the air) and water (drawn up from the soil) that is powered by the energy in sunlight. Six molecules of each are reorganised into one molecule of glucose, a simple sugary substance. The waste product is oxygen gas, which escapes from the leaves into the air. Almost all the oxygen in the air (which we breathe) was produced by a plant or other photosynthetic organism, such as a bacterium or alga.

Maggot-go-round

30 YEARS

Thankfully scientists have figured out a way for us never to run out of food. We can always eat maggots. Maggots adore human sewage, and grow nice and chubby after a few days of munching on poo. Luckily we don't have to eat the maggots ourselves. They are dried and crushed into powder and made into protein-rich pellets for farm animals. These then get slaughtered, we eat them and then the process starts all over again.

CONSERVATION

Biologists, experts in wildlife, are discovering more species all the time. Very often they find that the new species they have just discovered is very rare and in danger of extinction. About a third of all species are thought to be endangered. Let's take a look at how conservation will protect them in future.

Breeding back

15 YEARS

All farm animals and pets have been selectively bred. Over the centuries, humans have changed the way animals look by choosing which animals breed with each other. This ensures that all their offspring will have a certain feature. For example, dairy cows will all produce a lot of milk, while lap dogs are small and cuddly. The same system could be used to breed animals back from extinction! People could selectively breed closely related species for many years until they looked like the extinct variety. This is already being tried in South Africa, where an extinct type of zebra, called the quagga is being bred back from plains zebras.

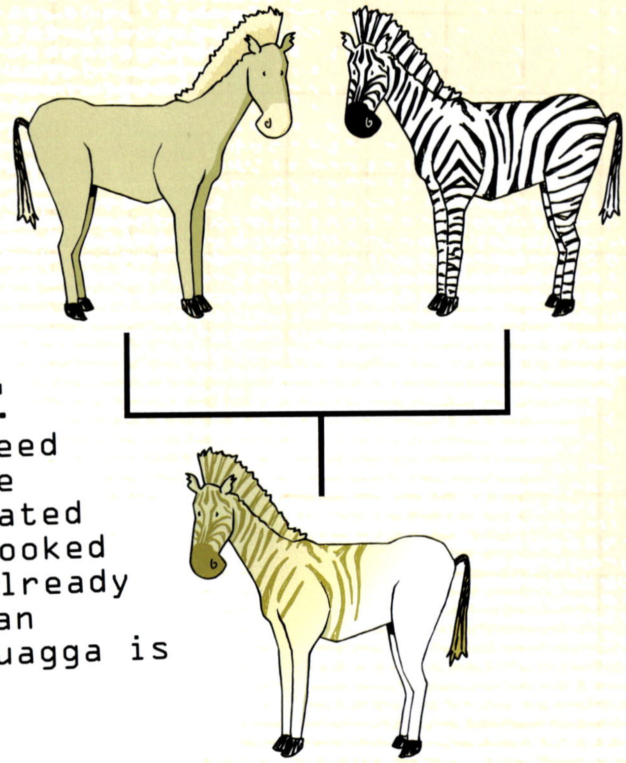

Droning on

5 YEARS

Small uncrewed, self-flying aircraft, or drones, could one day be sent to fly high over jungles, swamps and savannahs to watch over endangered animals. Solar-powered drones would never have to land and could send back information about how animals live. Drone surveillance could then track animals in remote areas to find out about their movements and so better protect them.

Clone rescue

5 YEARS

When a species becomes very rare, down to just a few individuals, it is sometimes best to capture them from the wild and keep them safe in zoos, to ensure that at least a few will survive. In future, we might not have to do that - we could take a sample of blood from a wild animal and keep it safe in a deep freeze. If the species died out, cloned versions could be bred in zoos and released into the wild. We could even clone animals that are already dead, by collecting a sample of the skin or hair.

Pollution patrol

10 YEARS

There are already robot cars, dogs, and even robot worms, and soon robot fish may be swimming around the coasts, on the lookout for pollution being dumped into the sea. If these seagoing pollution police find a ship pumping waste overboard or detect harmful chemicals coming out of a river, they can give an early warning before too much damage is done.

VIDEO CONSERVATION

5 YEARS

Primates and other intelligent animals living in zoos are healthier if they can interact with other animals. It helps them survive if they are ever returned to the wild. However, sending animals from one zoo to another for visits is very complicated. Perhaps technology could help. In future, animals around the world could watch and hear each other on live video screens.

ERROR ALERT

Learning to climb

Zoos often work together to breed large numbers of an endangered species and then return them to a safe wild habitat. One of the first species to benefit from this was the golden lion tamarin, a little monkey from South America. However, when the first tamarins were released into the wild, most of them fell out of the trees and died! Conservationists realised that the monkeys had grown up in cages with fixed perches, and they were not used to climbing in real trees with swaying branches. From then on, tamarins were only raised in enclosures with real trees.

CLIMATE CHALLENGES

Weather is just the everyday changes that happen in the atmosphere, which might be warm and dry one day, but cold and wet the next. When studied over many months and years, weather becomes known as the climate. It seems we are changing Earth's climate, making the weather more extreme, by adding carbon dioxide and other 'greenhouse gases' to the atmosphere. Climate change will be one of the biggest challenges for science and technology in the future.

Carbon capture

25 YEARS

It is natural for the air to contain small amounts of carbon dioxide, but over the last 250 years we have burned so much fuel that we have increased the amount by a third. And the amount of carbon dioxide is still going up, furthering climate change. One solution is to trap the carbon dioxide we produce so no more can get into the air. Like the oil and gas that we use for fuel, captured carbon dioxide could be transported in giant tankers and along pipes to be pumped back into old coal mines and oil wells.

Space shades

40 YEARS

If Earth gets too hot, it'll need to sit in the shade for a while. Thousands of folding parasols could be launched into orbit. Once in space, the parasols open up, shading Earth from the sun's rays.

Seeding the oceans

25 YEARS

Photosynthesising organisms thrive on carbon dioxide. They take it in from the air or water around them and turn it into food (see page 21). Geoengineers - scientists of the future who can alter Earth's climate - could add iron and other nutrients to the seas to create huge blooms of algae. These microscopic plankton would take huge amounts of carbon dioxide out of the air as they grow. The algae is eaten by shellfish, which put the carbon into their hard shells. The dead shells sink to the seabed and form limestones and chalks, locking the extra carbon away for ever as rock.

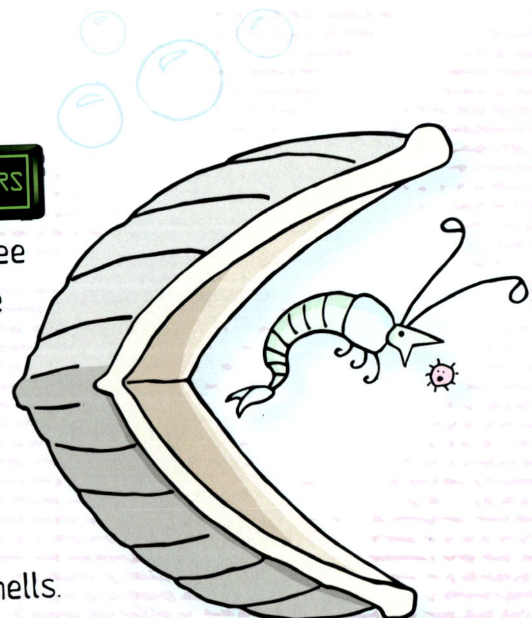

Going dim

25 YEARS

While adding carbon dioxide to the atmosphere makes it warm up, adding dust makes it cool down again. The dust helps clouds form and blocks out sunlight, so less heat gets into the air in the first place. Spraying ultrafine salt dust from fleets of aircraft or balloons might help to reverse climate change. However, this can only work if we also stop making the problem worse by releasing even more greenhouse gases into the sky.

Polishing the planet

40 YEARS

It is not direct sunlight that warms the greenhouse gases and creates climate change. Instead it is the heat that radiates back into the air from warm, sunbaked ground. Pale icy areas stay cold because they reflect the light straight back, so if we can make Earth more pale and shiny, it would cool it down. We could do this by covering empty areas, like deserts, with huge sheets of shiny plastic.

IT'S ELEMENTARY

Greenhouse effect

Earth's atmosphere creates a blanket of gas around the planet that traps heat. Bright sunlight warms the surface and then invisible heat radiates back into the sky. Most of that ends up out in space, but some is absorbed by the gases, especially the greenhouse gases such as carbon dioxide. We call them this because they work in the same way as the glass in a greenhouse – letting light in but stopping heat escaping. The 'greenhouse effect' is entirely natural, and without it, Earth would be a frozen planet covered in ice. However, humans adding greenhouse gases to the air appears to be warming the planet slightly, which may change the climate and make weather more extreme.

PAUSE FOR THOUGHT

One way to help solve climate change does not require technology. We could all burn less fuel. This would mean living less comfortable lives, eating fewer luxury foods, and seldom going on long journeys. Would this be better than trying to solve the problem with technology?

HEALTH AND SAFETY

The world today is safer than it has ever been. We are perhaps more aware of dangers – which can make us feel less safe – but knowing about potential problems means we can do something about them. In future, clever technology will make us safer still.

CRASH READY

15 YEARS

Imagine if your car knew when it was about to have a crash. A small radar signal sent out in all directions would alert it to another approaching vehicle. That might be just a fraction of a second before the collision, but that is enough time for the car to brace automatically for impact by tightening seat belts and sliding bars around the passenger cabin to divert the impact around them.

SAFETY CHIPS

10 YEARS

On building sites and in warehouses large objects are frequently on the move, and serious accidents can happen. In future, safety systems could monitor where all workers and vehicles are on the site. If they appear to be getting too close, everything is automatically shut down, averting an accident. The system would make use of wireless radio technology, such as RFID (radio-frequency identification) tags, to keep tabs on everything.

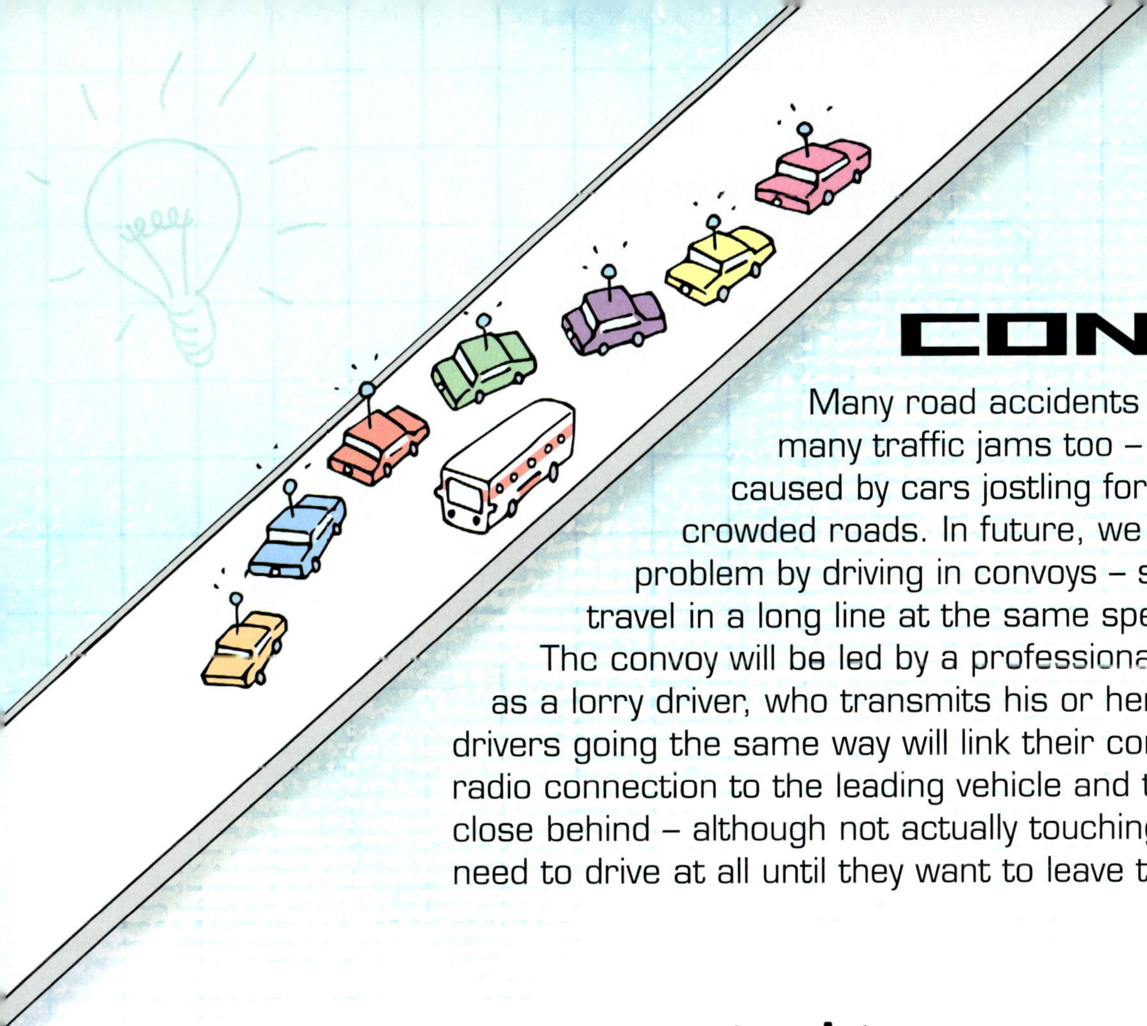

CONVOY!

10 YEARS

Many road accidents – and many traffic jams too – are caused by cars jostling for position on crowded roads. In future, we will reduce this problem by driving in convoys – so groups of cars travel in a long line at the same speed, like a train. The convoy will be led by a professional road user, such as a lorry driver, who transmits his or her destination. Other drivers going the same way will link their controls by a wireless radio connection to the leading vehicle and then travel along close behind – although not actually touching. They won't need to drive at all until they want to leave the convoy.

Transparent cockpits

20 YEARS

Every vehicle has some kind of blind spot where the driver or pilot cannot see. One day, we may all travel in transparent vehicles so we can see around us better. They will not be made of see-through plastic or glass. Instead the inside surfaces will be covered in screens with real-time videos of the outside displayed on them. This will mean that lorry drivers can look through their high doors to see people down the road or an airline pilot can see through the floor of the cockpit all the way to the ground.

COPYING NATURE

In the past, we have spent a lot of time and effort altering our natural surroundings to make an environment better suited to what we need – for building cities or growing food, for example. In future, we might do the opposite and try to build devices that copy the way nature does things. This idea is called biomimetics, meaning 'imitating life'.

Self-filling water bottle

15 YEARS

The fog beetles of Namibia live on the tallest sand dunes in the world. When they need a drink, there are no rivers or pools to sip from. Instead they climb to the top of the dunes and stand with their backs raised into the damp ocean wind. Droplets of moisture form on their skin, giving them just enough water to survive. A self-filling bottle is being developed that does the same thing: a small fan pushes air through the bottle and water droplets condense on the high-tech lining. In future all you'll need to carry is the bottle - the water will come out of thin air.

A fog beetle takes a drink.

Worm robot

20 YEARS

A soft-bodied, worm-shaped robot has been built that mimics the way a worm moves. Worms have not got bones or other hard body parts, so instead their muscles push against bags of liquid. That means a worm robot could squeeze into all kinds of tight places that people cannot reach. And the soft, squidgy body is pretty tough – a hammer blow would just bounce off.

Woodpecker shock absorber

15 YEARS

Engineers have copied the beak and skull of a woodpecker to make the ultimate shock absorber. Woodpeckers hammer dead wood so hard it creates a force 1000 times stronger than gravity - ten times as much as the human body can withstand. Copying the flexible materials in the bird's beak and skull has resulted in a shock-absorbing material so strong it even keeps working when fired from a gun into a wall. This material might one day protect sensitive electronics during accidents or be used to make super-tough body armour.

LIZARD-TONGUE TOOL

15 YEARS

Chameleons have long and sticky tongues used to snatch prey. Devices that need to grab objects, such as on factory production lines, could copy this system with sticky plastics on wires fired by electric motors. The problem solved by the chameleon (and copied by the robotic tongue) is to hit the target at the right speed – just hard enough to splat it and stick, but not so hard that it is whacked away in the opposite direction.

STACKS OF FACTS

Swimsuits designed to help people swim faster use the same trick as shark skin - tiny curved teeth all over the material literally cut through the water. The suits work so well, they are banned from top races.

The blades of wind turbines work better when they have little bumps along the edges. The idea came from the same kind of bumps, called tubercles, on the fins of humpbacked whales.

Velcro fasteners, invented in 1941, were inspired by the way burdock fruits use tiny hooks to cling to curly animal fur.

GLOSSARY

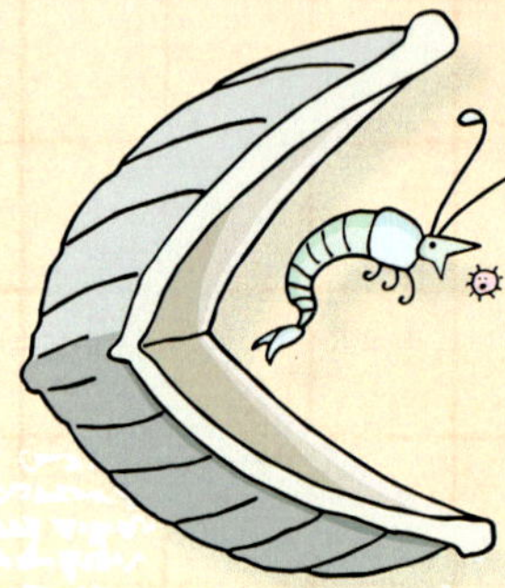

algae Tiny plant-like bugs that are too small to see without a microscope, but which photosynthesise in the same way as leafy plants. Algae live in water and other damp places.

artificial Made by people; the opposite of natural.

atom The smallest building block of a material. There are about 90 types of atom found on Earth, which combine to make all the things we see around us including our bodies.

climate change A process that is changing weather patterns around the world. Some of the changes are being caused by the gas pollution that people release into the atmosphere.

clone A animal that has been produced artificially with exactly the same set of genes as another older animal.

cocoon A protective layer around the body.

electronics An area of technology in which transistors, diodes and other components are used as switches to control the way electric current flows around a circuit. Generally the circuits are miniaturised onto microchips.

ferment A process that breaks chemicals down, releasing energy without using oxygen. Fermenting sugar makes alcohol, for example. Fermentation is normally performed by microscopic yeast and bacteria.

fertilisers Chemicals that are added to soil to help a plant grow. They are needed where the soil has run out of its natural supply.

gene Something that can be inherited, or passed down from parents to children. The gene is transmitted in the form of DNA.

membrane A very thin layer that divides something, often liquid. All living cells are surrounded by membranes.

molecules The smallest unit of a substance that is made up of a collection of atoms arranged in a certain way.

momentum A measure of the quantity of motion. Heavy objects have more momentum than lightweight ones, while fast-moving things have more momentum than slow objects.

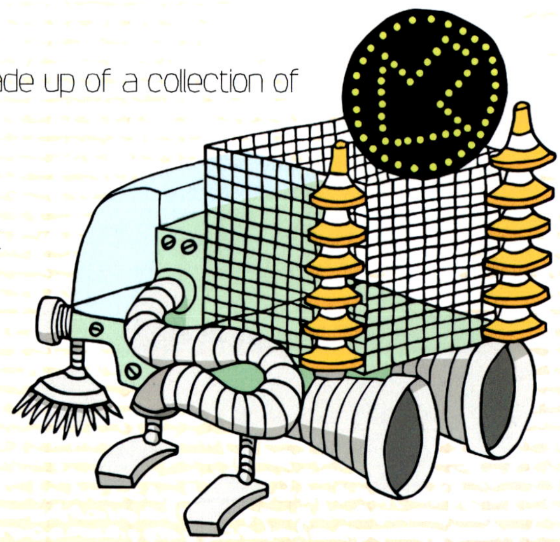

monorails A rail system where carriages run along a single rail or hang from it.

nanotubes Tubes formed by rolling sheets made from carbon atoms. Nanotubes are very strong even when they are very narrow.

nutrient A chemical that helps a plant, animal or other life form survive.

organism An individual form of life, such as an animal, plant or fungus.

parasol A sunshade umbrella.

plankton Tiny organisms that float or swim weakly through water.

pollution Chemicals that upset the balance of the natural environment. Light, heat and sound can also be seen as pollution.

radar A detection system that sends out radio waves and listens for their echoes to find out where objects are in the area.

RFID Stands for radio-frequency identification. RFID systems send out tiny radio signals that carry details about what they are.

technology Using scientific knowledge to make useful tools.

vaporise To turn material into a vapour or gas, usually by heating it.

USEFUL WEBSITES:

Find out more about climate change, how it is being caused, what it will do and what we can do about it.
www.epa.gov/climatestudents

Take a look inside Microsoft's Space of the Future for a few more ideas about how our homes will work in the near future.
www.bbc.co.uk/news/technology-21632855

See what it is like to join a platoon, or convoy of cars, in this video of a motorway system test.
www.youtube.com/watch?v=QYV7cqmaJ14

A blind man takes a driverless car for a spin thanks to Google
www.youtube.com/watch?v=cdgQpa1pUUE

Learn more about how scientists clone animals with this Click and Clone game.
learn.genetics.utah.edu/content/tech/cloning/clickandclone/

INDEX

accidents 26–27
AI (artificial intelligence) 7
air-traffic tracking
systems 14
aircraft 13, 14, 15, 23, 27
algae 8, 24
ammonia 10, 11
Antarctic 4, 16
Arctic 4, 10

biomimetics 28–29

car-bike 13
carbon dioxide 9, 10, 11,
20, 24, 25
cities 5, 12, 13, 16–17
climate change 5, 10,
24–25
clones 22
cocoons 6
conservation 22–23
convoys 27
countryside 4, 5

deserts 4, 12, 17, 25
driverless cars 12
drones 22

electricity 5, 8, 9
endangered species
22–23

farmbots 20
farming technology 20–21
fuels 5, 8, 10–11, 14, 18, 24

geothermal laser drilling 8
gravity 8
greenhouse
effect 25
gases 25

Haber process 11
health and safety 26–27
helicopters 12
home 6–7
hydrogen balls 10

ice roads 16
incinerators 18

light bulbs 7

maggots 21

nanotubes 16
natural habitats 4

OLEDs (organic light-
emitting diodes) 7
osmosis 19

parasols 17, 24
photosynthesis 21
pollution 5, 14, 15, 18, 23
power supplies 5, 8–9

recycling scanner 18
renewable energy 17
robot vehicles 11
robotic tongues 29
rocket planes 15
roller coasters 13
room stacks 6

sewage 19, 21
shock absorbers 29
Shweeb, the 12
solar panels 9
space junk 19

technology 6–7, 8–9, 20
teleportation 15
tidal reefs 9
towns 4, 16
transport 4, 12–13, 14–15
travel 12–13, 14–15
tsunamis 16
turbines 9, 29

waste 18–19
weeds 20
worm robots 28

zoos 22, 23